The Curvy Girl's Guide to Style

By: Chastity Garner
Illustration: Igigi.com

Library of Congress Control Number: LCCN: 2010905750
(paperback)

ISBN 1451560486
EAN-13 9781451560480

100 Enterprise Way
Suite A200
Scotts Valley, CA 95066

Illustration: Igigi, Igigi.com
Manuscript Editor: Ashley Easton
Graphic Design: Mindzai, www.mindzai.net
Photography: JFX Digital Photography, www.jfxdigital.com
Art Direction: Eve Harlowe Photography. www.eveharlowe.com

Dedication:

I dedicate my first book to my mom, Kat, and to my nephew, Christopher.
She gave up her dreams so I could achieve mine.
And to my nephew, I strive for my dreams
so I can help him to achieve his one day.

Contents

Introduction

I admire great style, and I'll openly admit that I keep tabs on all of the top stylists. I admire each of them for different reasons, but I recently noticed that none of them really shine when it comes to dressing plus-size women.

It's common knowledge that, traditionally, plus-sized women have always gotten the short end of the stick when it comes to fashion. Admittedly, "Dressing Plus-Size Women 101" is not taught in fashion schools as part of regular protocol. As a full-figured woman and stylist, (and one who has always been such,) I wrote this book to help guide, encourage, and inspire the inner stylistas in the many beautiful, curvy women out there. If you're reading this, I suspect you're one of them! By the end of this book, you should be able to style *yourself* into fabulousness every day.

And lucky for us, the mainstream fashion world is starting to change. Designers are starting to take notice of women with curves and have started to design stylish clothes for us, too. It's definitely time to finally embrace your curves, if you haven't already!

To give fair warning though, this book does contain a little tough love. I'm going to tell it you like a best friend (whose expertise and profession happens to be in style and fashion). Based on your particular body type, there will be certain things that shouldn't ever see the light of day, and other things that should be the building blocks of your entire wardrobe. Don't worry...it is all in love, because we're going to be making the world more stylish and confident...one curvy girl at a time. Get ready to look your best!

"Fashions fade; style is eternal"
Yves Saint Laurent

Chapter 9

Know Thyself

It's time to get naked...stark naked.

That said, you *may* want to make you sure you have a little bit of privacy. For this chapter, all you'll need is a full length mirror. If you're brave (or you can't find a moment's privacy in your own home), you can also do this in a dressing room. Just keep in mind if you go that route, you're not going to be in the most flattering of environments with all that harsh fluorescent light. So think twice before plotting a dramatic crash diet—*everybody* looks better in candlelight, even Halle Berry.

Okay, now, disrobe. It's time for you and your body to get reacquainted. Are you able to pinpoint your general proportions? What about your favorite figure features, and those other bits that always give you trouble when it comes to finding clothes? If you can, take note of them. This is the mannequin that you've been assigned for this crash course in curvy style!

You would think that if a woman lives with herself every day, she would know her body, the clothes that look best on her figure, and certainly something as basic as her own measurements. Surprisingly, I am constantly running into women who are not only unaware of their measurements, but do not have an idea of how to dress the bodies that they are in, either! Knowing your measurements, your body type, and the clothing pieces that work best for your body type is *essential* to cultivating great style.

Accurate measurements can be obtained from your local dry cleaner's or your alterations shop for a minimal cost—generally under five dollars. Having a grasp of your measurements is also important because it can help you determine where the majority of weight is carried on your body. Most of the fashionable plus-size clothing lines out there are available online, rather than in stores, so knowing your measurements will allow you to use the size charts provided by the website.

We all want to look gorgeous, and at the least, create the illusion of a perfectly curvy feminine silhouette. That's why it's important that we wear pieces that complement and balance out our unique figures. Which pieces will be blessings for your figure is largely determined by what sort of body shape you have. Of course, women come in numerous shapes and sizes. But there are a handful of basic body type categories into which most women should fall. And I'll talk a little bit about each of them next.

Pear Shape

lgigi.com

A lot of women tend to have this body type, myself included! The pear shape, aka the triangle, carries the majority of her weight on the hips, thighs, and buttocks. In other words, the pear-shaped woman tends to be a bit bottom-heavy. Pear figures generally have a small-ish bust, thin neck and a relatively slim face in comparison to the rest of her body, and their waists are usually well-defined.

The primary blessing of this body type is that it is very easy to create a curvy silhouette. Pears don't tend to have major stomach bulge issues, and they are sometimes able to wear dresses and tops that are not plus-size, thanks to a smaller upper body. The disadvantage to this body type directly relates to the where the weight is carried on the pear. Because the abundance of weight is carried on the hips, thighs, and buttocks, it can be extremely hard to find pants and jeans that fit. The waist is significantly smaller than the hips, which leaves the risk of sporting the much-loathed "plumber's crack." And ladies, plumber's crack is never okay. EVER! Not even with sexy panties! (*I descend from my soapbox.*)

Women with pear-shaped figures should definitely invest in dresses. Well-fitted pants are hard to find, and are simply not going to be as flattering as a skirt or a dress. The pear will likely look her most stunning in one of these two pieces. Contrary to popular belief, not only does the pear look fabulous in dresses with a fitted bodice that flare from the waist down, she can look amazing in more fitted dresses, too. However, this has to be done very carefully. With the wide hip span, a full girdle with a waist cincher or high waist panty may be necessary.

You might ask, *did she just say wear* two *girdles?* Yes, I did. The pear is very small from the belly button up, but this shape (like many others) can have a below-the-belly-button pouch, which may not be visible when wearing less form fitting styles, but it's very noticeable when wearing a dress that is fitted from the bust to knees.   A sure-fire way to see if you accomplished your goal is to check out your side profile in the mirror. If the side view is relatively flat along the front, then consider it mission accomplished.

When choosing tops for this physique, be aware that finding tailored tops that fit properly will be difficult because of the size of the hips. When a plus-size pear-shaped woman buys tailored tops off-the-rack, they often have to be taken to a seamstress for alterations to fit correctly.   For a quick fix, try tucking blouses into a high-waisted skirt until you can get them altered.

Since the pear shape's neck, shoulders, and bust are shapely and small compared to the lower half the body, strapless styles can look lovely. Try to focus on accumulating shirt styles that compliment the pear's lovely neckline and shoulders.   V-necklines are great for this, and shirts with ruffle embellishments will also bring attention to the upper portion of the body.

The waist is the pear figure's crowning glory, so emphasize it.   A belt or a sash accomplishes this brilliantly,   and is   quite flattering. An alternative tactic to give extra waist curvature is to incorporate vests. A vest that is fitted at the bust and waist can add that needed definition when you're looking for a belt substitute. Fill your wardrobe with pencil skirts, high-waist skirts, and flare skirts, which will allow you to easily incorporate belts. (More on belts later!)

Oversized tops or tops that hide the waist are bad news for pear-shaped ladies. Long peasant skirts can also look tent-like, since the pear if full on the bottom already. Shorts and miniskirts should not be in the wardrobe if you're a pear, either. Stick to hemlines that start at the knee.

When it comes to denims, I have heard some people advise against wearing skinny jeans for this body type and to choose wide-leg pants instead. I have both types of pants in my wardrobe, but I must say skinny jeans are my preference. Wide pant-legs on an ample, bottom-heavy woman can overwhelm the body and make it look larger than it is. A happy medium is to choose a boot cut jean. This jean gives you a fit that will hug your curves. I swear by the Lane Bryant Right Fit jeans. The blue circle jeans at LB are made for women with ample hips and a small waist. They tackle the dreaded gap in the back.

Most stylists will tell you to hide your hips and your rear end. I say *embrace*. Yes, you'll be showcasing some incredible curves, and done the right way your curves can be quite lovely and eye-catching. Moderation is *key* when it comes to showing off your assets. No one should be a sex kitten every day and no one should be June Cleaver every day, either.

Hourglass Shape

The easiest body type to dress is the hourglass. If you have the good fortune to possess this body type, consider yourself lucky—you're the envy of virtually all womankind. The hour glass shape describes a woman whose bust and hip measurements are close in number, with her waist being about ten inches less than her bust and waist. The waist is clearly defined, with body weight balanced above and below. When The Commodores referred to "36-24-36," they were talking about this enviable figure.

A great feature of the hourglass body type is that it is proportional. Most modeling agencies are looking for women that are proportional, and the majority of plus-size clothes are made to fit this physique. So of all the body types, you have the easiest time shopping with the least amount of alterations. The hourglass figure has a lot of options and just so you know, yes, we are all jealous.

Accentuating the waist is a no-brainer tactic for this body type. This can easily be done with wide or skinny belts. Like the pear shape, the hour glass can wear fitted dresses with full skirts. Because the face and neck are relatively slim, accentuating them with an open collar shirt or a V-neck top will compliment this body type wonderfully. Pencil, flare, and A-line skirts all look great on hourglasses, as well as most dresses, like A-line, wrap, and fitted styles.

Given the vast options for the hourglass, there is still one no-no that you need to be aware of. This body type should avoid oversized clothes. Oversized tops and baggy pants will make you look shapeless! That being said, longer, looser tunics have been rather popular lately. The key here is to pursue balance. So if you're going to throw on a breezy, loose top, pair it with leggings and some heels, and maybe a belt!

Hourglasses can wear the bootcut, skinny, and wide leg jeans and look great. Bootcut & skinny jeans show off her curves and can slim down the frame. Because of her proportionate frame, wide leg jeans look totally chic on her, but beware of wide leg jeans with *too* much volume. They actually make the hourglass look heavier and create the illusion that her hips and thighs are bigger than they really are.

Upside-down Triangle Shape

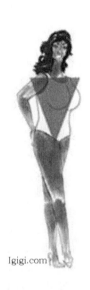

Igigi.com

The upside-down triangle-shaped woman has wide shoulders and carries most of her weight in the upper body. Because of the width of her shoulders, she often has a short neck, large bust, and small hips and thin legs. Balancing the top and bottom is the objective for this physique.

The great thing about this body type are the beautiful, shapely and toned legs, which allows this woman to be able to wear shorter hemlines than the average curvy girl. Clothes that work best for this body type include wide leg pants and jeans, V-neck tops, and A-line dresses. Your goal should be to create a proportional look. Wear wide legs pants to balance out the top half of the body with the bottom half. V-neck and scoop-neck tops can help create the impression of an elongated neck. When wearing a dress, go with the A-line silhouette, which will work with your body to create the appearance of an hourglass figure. The shift dress also looks great, because it starts out small at the shoulders and expands outwards into an upside down V-shape, creating a proportionate look.

When wearing shirts, make sure you look concentrate on blouses that fit the bust, curve over and under the bust, and then fit the midsection. A shirt that fits you in this way will help give the appearance of a curvy, nipped-in waistline. Don't let your ample breasts camouflage your potential curves. Above all, avoid skinny jeans, pencil skirts, turtlenecks, and shoulder pads. Skinny jeans & pencil skirts draw attention to the imbalance of the shape, diverting more attention to the difference in size between the upper and lower body. Turtlenecks and any other tops with high collars can draw attention to the lack of neck length. Shoulder pads will heighten your shoulders and make your neck look short. When buying a blazer with a shoulder pad, remove it! Got puffy sleeves with pads? Remove those too! Belting should only occur with this body type when wearing a dress or skirt that flares from the waist-down.

Women with an upside down triangle shape (or just large busts in general) should be careful with shirts that have a seam to emphasize the bust. Often, I have seen women wear these tops and instead of the seam riding right below the bust where it is supposed to be, the seam rests in the middle of the bust. This can give you a very unflattering look and the seam in the middle of the bust will flatten you out and make you look smushed. An additional disadvantage? These types of tops tend to rise up as you are going along with your day. So although it may fit fine when you left home, you could end up trying to tug the darn thing down all day long. To avoid this, you can do several things. First, make sure you have a push up bra that will keep your breasts in place. Try tops that have stretch to help. Before you leave the house, walk around, get up, sit down, and check yourself in the mirror to see if your top is still in place. If it is, you're good to go!

Box Shape

The box-shaped lady has close to even measurements in the bust, waist, and hip. Like the upside-down triangle shape, this figure also tends to have a short neck. Her best features are toned arms and legs. It can be quite a challenge to create a feminine silhouette, since the waist is not clearly defined. However, don't fret over this! Since the area underneath the bust is the smallest part of any woman, cinching and belting this can actually give even the box shape the appearance of having a defined waistline.

lgigi.com

The benefits of this figure, as mentioned above, are the shapely and toned limbs. I hear all the time from women that are deathly afraid of showing their arms. You ladies with the box shape do not have this issue, so let's show them off! Wear sleeveless tops and shorter hemlines to show off those arms and legs.

Dresses that have waist definition, whether at the natural or empire waist, can help to create a curvy shape. Box-shape figures can try tiered, A-line, and high waist flare skirts to create a defined waist. Dresses with a peplum flare also look stunning on this figure. Peplum dresses are one of the easiest dresses for any body type to wear—they automatically form curves and they are extremely forgiving on the tummy area. (And if you haven't heard of peplum dresses, Google it, ladies! You'll be glad you did!)

Necklines that are open and plunging can help to make the neck look longer on this figure, while sweetheart necklines will give the illusion of some feminine curve. Steer clear of turtlenecks to prevent the neck from looking short and the shoulders from looking wide. Also avoid extremely fitted dresses, such as the tube dress. A plain, tight fitting dress will only magnify the lack of variation between the bust, hip, and waist measurements. Instead, go for fitted garments with a gathered or ruched waist.

Boot cut, dark denim jeans are an essential for this body type. These jeans help create some serious feminine curvature from the hip down. Since the body type tends to have a slender side profile, bring attention to such wonderful lines by wearing flat front pants.

Apple Shape

The apple shape is characterized by her full bosom, full midsection, slim hips, slender legs, and semi-broad shoulders. This body type faces the challenge of defining a waist when there is little or no waist definition. Following some key suggestions, though you'll be able to enhance your waist curvature.

The "go-to" dress for the apple is the wrap dress. It creates sexy curves while showing off the bust. Any skirt that flares out from the waist down will look dazzling on the apple. Wearing a top tucked into a flared skirt can be a charming look. Try shorter hemlines to show off your slender legs. Avoid empire waist dresses, though—they can make you look pregnant.

lgigi.com

Tops for the apple shape can look extremely sexy—sometimes too sexy! This physique's ample bust can be the talk of the town, but we want it to be for the right reason. Showing just enough cleavage is the mark of a stylish lady, showing too much can make people wonder if you're trying to sell something! I have literally seen women's breasts so far out that they look as if they were getting ready to nurse a baby. To ensure you don't expose your girls too much, take a look in the mirror. For some ladies, a sign that too much of our cleavage is showing is being able to see the veins that reside around the nipple area. Another way you can tell too much of your bust is out is the two-finger check. At minimum, you should be able to fit two fingers from the start of your areola to the neckline of the blouse. The third and final test you can try is the jump test. Hop a minimum 5 times (yes, I am very serious), if a nipple is close to becoming visible or a boob pops out, your blouse is definitely cut too low. Throw on a camisole underneath or change tops to correct the situation.

The apple's shoulders allow her to carry off lovely embellished neckline. Keep your eye on blouses that accent your bosom's curves, but don't let the cleavage pour out. One shoulder or asymmetrical blouses can do just that. The one shoulder helps to break up the the width of the shoulders, while allowing just enough cleavage to show. The off the shoulder top can also flatter this neckline while minimizing the bust. When baring your shoulders, don't forget to give that adorable over-the-shoulder glance to the cutest guy in the room. It gets them every time.

It is necessary for all body types to have good bras, but it is particularly crucial for the apple to have one that fits properly and supports her bust correctly. The bra will be the foundation for her outfits and thus set the tone for her and how she is perceived. Whether we like it or not, the elevation of the bust is extremely important when conveying the age of a woman. A high bust line will mean that a woman looks younger, a low bust line will make the woman look older. To achieve the desired "altitude" some women have been known to resort to the drastic measure of wearing two bras. Later, we will dive more into bras and foundation garments, but I do want to communicate the importance of a great bra for this body type in particular. A tip to keep your bust at the right height is when you feel them slipping, find a private area, bend over, pull your bra away from your chest and do a quick shimmy. This will put your breasts back in the proper place.

Whatever your body type, there is great style out there for you. All these guidelines may feel overwhelming in the beginning, but grab a highlighter, honey, and work it out. The main rule is to define your waist. Waist definition creates cleaner lines and gives you that oh-so-feminine magnetism. If you feel like you fall between the categories of more than one body type, don't worry. As I said at the beginning of this chapter there could literally be hundreds of different body types. Although you should lean toward the style advice geared towards the main body type that you fall under, take little tidbits from the other types that relate to you. This will allow you to customize your do's and don'ts based on your specific figure traits.

Chapter 2

Ten Essentials for the Curvy Girl's Wardrobe

During my years of styling, I've come to the conclusion that every woman's wardrobe needs, more or less, ten essential pieces. These pieces can provide endless possibilities to your closet, allowing you to go from work to a night out on the town, to casual shopping on the weekend. Before I let you in on the curvy girl's 10 essential pieces you must promise me something. If you decide to go out and purchase some of these pieces, you should take the curvy girl's oath. Okay, hold up your right hand and repeat after me:

I, (insert name), promise to invest in these pieces. I also promise to take care of these pieces to the best of my ability for their longevity, even if this means dry cleaning trips and/or trips to the seamstress. I promise this for as long as I live or until I get too old to leave the house, then I will get my children to complete the tasks for me.

The purpose of this oath is let you know how important it is to invest in these ten essentials. When you invest in these pieces, certainly keep within your budget, but just the same, your essential pieces *should* be among the highest quality items in your wardrobe. Reason being is that you will wear them more than any other pieces in your closet. Think to yourself, how many times do you wear a pair of black trousers in a work week? Now I won't tell anyone, but I *know* some of you have been wearing those trousers up to three times a week. The better the quality of these essentials, the more likely the piece is to last and stay looking like new.

Now, without further ado, here are the ten essential wardrobe pieces for the curvy girl:

1. *Foundation garments*

Later I will dedicate an entire chapter to the ins and outs of foundation garments and girdles. Why, you ask? It's because they are SO...CRITICALLY...IMPORTANT! Do you know what I would look like in a curve-hugging dress without my foundation? I shudder at the mere thought! With the proper girdle, you can create clean lines on the body, flatten out that middle, and smooth down any extra hip. And no whining about them not being comfortable, ladies. When is the last time your stilettos have been comfortable? Uh-huh, that's what I thought. And actually, some of the newer foundation garments aren't all that bad, if you find the specific type you need, and get it in the proper size. My favorite foundation garments have come from Lane Bryant and Spanx, but for you budget-istas out there, a trip to your local TJMaxx or Ross can turn up good foundation garments for a fraction of the price.

2. *A black skirt*

A versatile black skirt that fits well is great for any working girl's wardrobe. The right style skirt gives off the look of class and sophistication. Don't tie yourself down to the pencil skirt, because as you know from Chapter

1, it does *not* flatter every body type. The critical thing about choosing a skirt is selecting the cut that works best for you, not the skirt that everyone says you should have in your closet. Select between the flare, A-line, and pencil. Avoid the straight skirt because it usually makes you look really boxy or really wide. The essential skirt should hit somewhere between mid-knee to right below the knee. The correct fit of a pencil should be close the body, wider at your hip area, and a bit tighter closer to the knees. If you have issues with the back of your legs or don't like the splits in the back you can easily take it to a seamstress to get them closed up.

Now, aside from the initial logistics of finding a good fit, a simple black skirt can be a very sexy yet classic item to have in your wardrobe, outlining the natural curves or creating balanced proportion. For example, if you have a post-work event and need to make a quick change after your day at the office, pair your skirt with a strapless top and a cardigan, a skinny belt, your cutest secretary shoes, and your boyfriend's watch. When you go to a dinner party afterwards, just ditch the cardigan, add a large belt, jeweled clutch, and strappy sandals with a heel. In a matter of seconds you'll look ready for after-hours play!

3. *Black trousers or pants*

What woman doesn't love her black pants or doesn't wear them at least once a week? Black pants that fit properly can be *so* chic. If you are in that dressing room and you find that pair of black pants that are "magic," grab *two or three pairs*, girl, because you might not ever find that perfect pair again. If necessary, hem and alter those pants to fit you perfectly, and they will look like you paid twice as much for them.

4. Black leggings

I know I am going to get some disagreement on this one, but in my opinion, God didn't create a more comfortable, chic wardrobe staple than black leggings. And what's even better is a good pair that feature a bit heavier fabric and a tight stretch so that it can act as a light foundation garment for your lower body. Leggings are great for the dress that may be a little too short for comfort, for cold winter days when you really want to wear a dress, or for a weekend outfit paired with that cute long tank top you have.

You can even incorporate them in your office wear as a twist on the opaque tights look. Try pairing leggings with your favorite sweater dress and your favorite knee-high boots. The general rule for leggings is to keep the butt area covered, because when you deal with spandex, there's a fine line between looking great and looking, well, not-so-great.

Since leggings are so popular now, they come in different prints and colors. I have yet to see any woman, with the exception of Amber Rose, look good in pair of metallic leggings. Actually, metallic anything on the lower region of your body is a bad idea. Plus-size ladies should also steer clear of liquid leggings—the ones with the slight sheen that make them look like they're wet. These leggings will not only draw attention to any imperfections in your butt and legs, but they will amplify them. There may be a few women who have the perfect legs and bottoms for these leggings, but they are few and far in between. So if you have to question whether you should wear them, when you're initially trying them on, you probably shouldn't.

Leggings are a great way to express your individual style, whether in black, solid colors, or even in tie dye. Remember to look out for any cellulite, lumps, and bumps while trying on bright colored leggings—any minor imperfections are more likely to show if the leggings aren't black. But hey, if you've tried on a pair of purple tie dye leggings and they look fab, go for it!

5. A *little black dress, a.k.a. the L.B.D.*

Without a doubt every woman needs at least one little black dress, but in my candid opinion, the more the merrier! This is your "go-to" item any variety of situations. When you don't have anything to wear, you can throw a L.B.D. and feel much better. Likewise, when you want to look stunningly sexy, choose a L.B.D. with a sumptuous fabric and elegant tailoring. This dress saves the day in a crunch and can even, with the right accessory change, transition from your office to your night of dancing over the course of even a quick cab ride. (My New York curvy girls *know* what I am talking about!)

The L.B.D. is timeless. The one that you take home from the store should accentuate the most gorgeous parts of your body. If you have great legs, then your LBD may be a little shorter than the standard knee-length hem. If your waist is small, then your L.B.D. could be cinched at the waist. If you have great shoulders and a long neck then your L.B.D. can be strapless. Whatever your favorite feature, your L.B.D. should show it off.

I have two places in which I regularly look for my L.B.D.s. I know I can go to David's Bridal to find a structured L.B.D. with minimum embellishments. Another plus of shopping here is that if you need some alteration done on the dress, David's Bridal has an alteration shop on-site. For my more glamorous L.B.D.s I rely on the plus size designer label Jibri (www.jibrionline.com). It is a little costlier than your average alteration shop on the corner, but the designs are unique, distinguished and totally fabulous.

Style tip - Don't think you can't take your L.B.D. from night to day? With a few simple steps you can transfer this look to the workplace. Go for sophisticated pumps instead of strappy sandals or super-high heels. Add a blazer or cardigan to tone down the neckline of the dress if it is low cut or strapless. Then put up your hair and throw on your favorite pearls to complete the office look.

6. A *crisp, white, button-down collar shirt*

I know that this one can be little tricky for the curvy girl. I love a white shirt, but because most curvy women don't have an hourglass figure, the white shirt can create a bit of a dilemma. But this doesn't mean you should go without. When you're looking for a white shirt, find one that fits the largest part of your upper body, whether it is your breasts, hips, or belly. Any seamstress will tell you it is easier to tailor down than tailor up. So once you find nice a shirt that fits the largest part of your body, have the shirt tailored in to the smaller portions of your upper body. This will take your white shirt and turn it into one of your most favorite pieces. Wearing a crisp white shirt always exudes classiness and understated good taste.

White shirts are typically easiest to find at your local department store. Most designers that carry plus-sizes, if they make nothing else, always make a white blouse. My personal favorite is from Lauren by Ralph Lauren. Every season consists of at least one high quality white button up shirt for the curvy girl.

7. A *trench coat*

If you've seen *The Devil Wears Prada,* you'll certainly remember the scene where Andy is walking through New York in one of her oh-so-chic new outfits, straight from the sample closet of the runway. What you should notice more than anything else is that her outfit was built around a great long coat. During the early spring and the fall the trench coat is an essential piece that you could be wearing out and about nearly every day. The trench coat is a great outfit saver because it can give you a sophisticated look, even if you look like a mess underneath. Not that I *ever* advise looking like a mess at any time, but you know, sometimes life happens.

My picks for that spring/fall coat is a one that hits right above the knee and creates a feminine shape. Belted trench coats accomplish this particularly well. Again, fit is always a factor when choosing a trench coat. Remember, since the coat will have to fit you from the knee to the shoulders pick a coat that fits the largest parts of you and then tailor down. Don't buy one that's too tight through the arms or shoulders, because this can seriously hamper your movement and look decidedly uncomfortable. I do need to confess something, though—my dirty little secret, and a great curvy girl tip. I *do,* in fact, have coats that I will *never* be able to button over my hips. They fit my upper body perfectly and still look cute, but I just have to wear them open. Try it—you may be pleasantly surprised!

8. A *day dress*

A day dress is a casual dress that can be rocked at brunch with the ladies or on a stroll through downtown. This dress is casual but always flattering. My day dress of choice at the moment is the shirt dress. It gives the crisp sophisticated look of a button up shirt, but is light and airy enough that you could take a casual stroll through the park, and look (and feel) perfectly at home.

Wrap dresses are especially great for jet-setting curvy girls, because many shirt dresses are made with jersey, which doesn't wrinkle and is highly versatile. The wrap dress also looks great on almost any body because it makes your waist look like the smallest part of your body. Since the waist of a wrap dress is adjustable, even if you have some moderate weight gain or loss, the dress will still fit. This is a great dress to check the standard-size stores for—one of my favorite wrap dresses is actually from Banana Republic! Since shirt dresses are generally a single piece of fabric that you wrap to fit your body, tag size isn't the "end-all, be-all" when trying to find one that works for you.

Don't overlook other daytime styles. Sundresses are also great for showing off a summertime chic look, not to mention sweet sun-kissed shoulders. Many of these lately are being designed with elastic smocking on the back, so a good fit is almost guaranteed.

Style tip: Your wrap dress, like your L.B.D., can transition from day to night (or night to day) with just a few minor changes. For daytime, add a camisole if the neckline is too low. Select a complementary pair of flats, and a hobo bag, and you're ready for the day. For night, add a pair of peep toe patent leather pumps, ditch the camisole and add a funky jeweled clutch and a couple of chunky bangle bracelets.

9. A *blazer*

A blazer can often save the day by adding that perfect finishing touch to your outfit. A great-fitting blazer will give you a put-together look whether you are in the grocery store or on a business luncheon. Fit is key for adding this item to your wardrobe. Beware the too-tight blazer, but also avoid the oversized blazer.

I know the boyfriend blazer is all the rage right now. Curvy girls can work this trend, too, but remember to still work your curves by adding a skinny belt or closing a button to give a little waist definition. This is definitely an item worth getting tailored to achieve that perfect fit that says "money."

10.   *Dark denim jeans*

Dark denim jeans are a chameleon in the wardrobe. They can be easily dressed up or down, and they're wonderfully versatile. That's why they're on this list! However, finding a pair of jeans is sometimes easier said then done. Plus-size or not, the hunt for a pair of jeans that have the optimal fit can have you wandering in and out of fitting rooms for months. First, narrow down the options by trying the style(s) that best suit your body type. The styles in question are skinny, bootcut, and wide leg.

Regardless of the style, all your jeans should fit your frame. Baggy jeans make your butt look shapeless and/or create the look of a "man crotch." Jeans that are too tight at the waist can give you the dreaded muffin-top. If you get stuck in the situation where you get caught between sizes, (let's say size 18 is too small and size 20 is too big,) choose the size up, as it will allow for simple alterations and give you a better fit. Alterations can also help you avoid embarrassing, un-ladylike wardrobe malfunctions like plumber's crack.

Pocket details are also important. Pockets that are too small can make the derriere look extremely wide and no pockets can allow the world to see all the imperfections of your butt, unless, of course, you have a great butt. Stick to a decent size pocket—about as big as your hand—for maximum butt-appeal.

When it comes to the length of your jeans, look for an inseam length that will allow you to wear both heels and flats. Sporting jeans that are too long make your legs look super short. Jeans that are too short...well, it's just not a good thing. That's why we have capris, not too-short jeans. You can actually play with varying lengths a bit when it comes to skinny jeans, but when buying your essential pair, choose an ankle-length pair or longer, so that your jeans can get you through the winter months.

You can approach buying jeans in a couple of ways. One way is to buy jeans to fit the largest part of your body and tailor down. Remember you can tailor any part of the jeans—from the crotch to the waist to the length. Another way to approach this dilemma is to buy body type-specific jeans. I personally swear by Lane Bryant jeans. They make jeans for specific body types; the pear, the hourglass, and the apple. The jeans that I bought there fit like a glove, and that's such an amazing feeling! PZI & Cookie Johnson Jeans are also labels that cater to the women with some curve to contend with. Their jeans go up to a size eighteen and have about a ten-inch difference between the waist and the hip.

Low rise jeans can create many issues for the curvy girl, no matter your particular shape or size. Low rise will do one of two things. For the apple figures, they could allow your stomach to hang out over your jeans. (Yuck. Just don't buy that pair if it creates this particular effect!) Hourglass, box shapes, and pears will run into problems with their hips coming out over the waistband if they're too snug. And unfortunately, plumber's crack is almost inevitable with low rise jeans. If you do decide that you just can't live without your low rise jeans remember a couple things. A belt around the waist of the jeans is necessary to keep them from sliding downwards. Also, if your jeans have gotten too small, you *need* to let them go, because they're going to make you look bigger than you really are. Jeans that fit = flattering silhouette.

Beyond the ten essentials, there are a few other basic, high-utility items that will look great on you regardless of whether they are in or out of the current trends.

Jean jacket. Feeling overdressed? The jean jacket is great for taking any outfit down a notch. Throw it on and look casual chic.

Sweater Dress. Form-fitting and belted, the sweater dress adds a hint of sexy and dash of style. This a great piece to pick up from your local thrift store. Regardless of the size on the tag, sweater dresses tend to fit a large range of size.

Cardigan. The most delightful material is cashmere, if it fits in your budget. It will last longer and keep its shape better. Pair it with your favorite pencil skirt for the office or with a pair of jeans for a date at the movies.

Turtleneck. These are sexiest on long-necked curvy girls. A fitted turtleneck and a pair of skinny jeans can give you that sleek look, but don't forget about the foundation underneath!

Camisole. This piece is great for adding a little extra length on your top. It looks superb underneath sheer blouses. Camisoles can function to add a hint of color to an outfit. They can also make you more comfortable in a top that you think may be a tad too short, or cut a bit too low in the neckline.

A touch of leopard print. Whether it is a blouse or skirt, animal print can be fabulous, but *do* be wary. Less is always more with this print. All you need is a pop of it! My personal favorite leopard skirt came from the Atlanta-based plus labels Jibri. Let's just say that I turn heads whenever I wear it! Make sure you don't walk out of the house wearing leopard from head to toe (or any animal print for that matter!) That's never a good idea.

When shopping for your essentials it is important to not buy pieces that are too trendy or overly-embellished. These pieces can look dated after a just short amount of time. Pick natural materials that are classic, like cotton, silk, satin, and wool. These will look better and last longer than synthetic fabrics.

Swimsuits

Although not considered to be a part of the essentials, every woman does need a flattering swimsuit for vacation getaways, tanning, and plain old poolside relaxing. Now we all know swimsuit season can be scary. You walk into that dressing room and you see all the fruits (or donuts) of your labor from the entire year. Some years, it's enough to make you gasp in shame. But hold your head up high; plus-size swimsuits have come a *long* way. They're still not all perfect (or magic) but if you buy a quality swimsuit that fits the needs of your body type you can come out looking like a star. Girlfriends, be warned! This is a tough love section, so if you're not up for it right now, you might want to proceed to the next chapter.

First, you need to accept that this swimsuit season you will be buying a plus-size bathing suit. Once you have passed over the threshold of curviness (size 14+) do not try to wear skinny girl bathing suits. Just because the suit is made with spandex or Lycra does not mean there's no limit to how much you should try to stretch the swimsuit. Yeah you can probably get into the suit, but is it really a good idea for a full bottom piece to look like a thong? Not to mention, it's not exactly an ego booster, either.

Before you hit the stores, make sure you've taken your measurements and have identified your body type. Assess your problem areas and choose the suits you try on accordingly:

For you curvy girls with tummy issues, make sure to look for swimsuits that have ruching in the waist area. The gathering will give the illusion of a flatter stomach area, and it will imperceptibly camouflage any bumps or folds.

Ladies with a large bust will find the best support from swimsuits with an underwire. Soft cups provide the next best support. The bustier curvy girl should also pay attention to the back of a swimsuit. Crisscross straps and a razor back will provide better bust support than and open back or U shaped back.

For pear--shaped ladies, look for a straight skirt, shorts, or a sarong wrap. Embellishments up top can draw attention to your delicate neckline and smaller bust, and give a little more balance to your shape.

Bikinis, as a general rule, aren't for us curvy gals. (Unless you're, you know...like plus-size supermodel Crystal Renn.) Work with that one-piece or tankini. None of your friends want to be the one to tell you that the two-piece bikini you've been eying since March is a mistake, so don't put them in an awkward position. Consider yourself told.

One more thing: cheap bathing suits are a no-no! In case you don't know, even straight size girls pay a chunk for quality swimsuits, and they are small. Why? Because a thicker, well-constructed suit is going to compliment their bodies more than a cheap suit that is thin and shapeless. The same goes for you. A good suit will last you a couple years, and it will flatter you significantly more than a cheap one. Remember, some swimsuits now come with tummy and body slimmers that will make you look your personal best.

Ultimately, your options are limited in the world of plus-size bathing suits for the time being. Face it and move on. Work with what is being offered. And if you just can't make a decision on a suit buy, a black full piece swimsuit will always look sleek and sophisticated.

Quick tips:

Stay away from the old lady dress swimsuit. My ladies under 40, stay away from the ruffly skirts on your swimsuit. They'll age you. Go with some terry cloth shorts, a cute sarong or, if you must, do a straight skirt. You will get the same coverage but without that frumpy old-lady skirt fluttering around your thighs.

Examine the fabric of a swimsuit to make sure it is thick. This is probably the most important rule. Thin fabric can be transparent-looking and show all of your body's flaws.

Play up your summer look with accessories. Grab some large glasses, a cute sarong or tunic, a fabulous beach bag, some lovely sandals, and you'll be ready to make your debut at the pool.

When you go shopping for all of these basic wardrobe pieces, have your body type tips in your head, so you can purchase the right styles for your closet. As your wardrobe essentials grow, watch your "I don't have anything to wear" days dwindle. Mixing in these pieces with trendy attire can yield virtually countless looks, and will allow you to reinvent your wardrobe time and time again.

Ladies, I do *not* advocate having a boring closet. Remember, black is not the only color out there. Yes it is the most slimming and we all love it, but you don't want to look like you have a membership to Club Funeral. Have fun with stripes, plaids, prints, and florals. Play with different colors to get a refreshing look and complement the wonderful features that you have. Color and patterns can infuse your wardrobe with your own unique personality and convey to the world what you're all about. With a little practice, you'll look fabulous in no time.

Chapter 3

Foundations, Girdles, and Brassieres, Oh My!

To reinforce the importance of undergarments, I'm going to spend a whole chapter talking about your underwear. That's right! When I started blogging, I was surprised at how many questions I got about girdles. For me, foundations have always been a part of my life. They were introduced to me by my mother at a relatively young age. I remember her telling me I should wear foundations to avoid what she described as "distasteful jiggle." I can remember looking in the mirror at thirteen, and seeing the difference between my tummy with a girdle on and without one. I made the decision then that foundations would be a part of my everyday life just because I look so much sleeker with them on.

Now let's have a little girl-to-girl pow-wow. Foundations, girdles, and even bras, for that matter, are not very comfortable. I've even gotten bruises and scratches from my undergarments, all in the name of fashion and because I want to look my best. If you are looking for comfort, fashion may not be your forte. Glamorous clothing is never comfortable. Our party clothes are binding (as Cher from *Clueless* said), our pumps hurt like hell, and who doesn't let out a sigh of relief once your bra is removed after a long day? I'm a card-carrying member of the small booby club and I even do that. And just so you know, skinny girls wear various shaping garments, too. They may not wear them as often as a plus-size girl, but they do have them! So throw out that whole notion of "if they don't have to wear them, neither do I."

Being plus-size is fine, but being sloppy (at any size) is not. In the spirit of being helpful, I am obliged to mention the stomachs I have seen hanging out over pants, multiple back rolls, cellulite showing through poorly-chosen fabrics, and just endless fashion tragedies that didn't have to happen.

I am not just talking about my plus-size ladies, either. Hold on to your girdles, because it's story time. I was once at a little soirée with some of the who's who in Atlanta and saw a female celebrity. I won't say names, but this woman could have worn no more than a size eight, if that. She had on a white dress and a thong underneath. The dress was pretty tight and a little transparent. But the woman's thong was not the issue at all. It was the texture of her behind. The poor woman's cellulite was extremely visible because it was highlighted by a skin-tight jersey knit white dress with nothing but a thong underneath. My point with this story is that every woman needs to have a foundation garment or two in her arsenal. Some need to wear them more often than others, but every woman needs one for at least certain fashion situations.

The main reason to wear foundation garments is to help sculpt a feminine silhouette. You will hear me refer to this again, so listen up. The desired shape for any woman is a basically an hourglass. Often times our bodies are not exactly set up that way, and foundation garments help create those curvy lines. Remember that everyone will have a different result with foundations. Don't expect the extreme "coke bottle figure" if that's not your body type, but you can certainly expect to achieve an appearance of a relatively defined waist. And this should be your goal, especially as a curvy girl.

There are several types of foundation garments, and depending on what your needs are, this will determine the type of foundation garment you will need. I tend to look at Spanx first for my girdle needs. They carry a wide variety of different types of foundations that work with a multitude of garments. There are many different types of girdles and sometimes finding the exact one you need can take some looking around. The basic types of foundation garments are described below:

Camisole - This top can help minimize the bust and back fat, and will flatten the tummy area somewhat. It's designed for a woman who is top-heavy and doesn't have ample hips. If you have ample hips this, girdle could roll up, rendering it pretty much useless.

High Waist Panty - This is great for keeping the stomach held in and somewhat flat. It also assists with the taming of back fat because it comes as high as your bra closure. I use this one under high waist flare skirts, pencil skirts, and even with a jeans and t-shirt combo.

High waist short – For the hippy girl with large thighs, this foundation garment helps with forming a curvy silhouette and dealing with cellulite on the butt and thighs. This one also helps with keeping in the stomach and to control some back fat. It is an excellent girdle under trousers, leggings, and form fitting dresses. I personally have issues with finding a girdle to fit my hips and hold my stomach in. I often wear a high waist panty girdle with this for that extra support in the stomach area. You can infer from this that it is okay to come up with your own shapewear combo that caters to your individual shaping needs.

Waist cincher – Waist cinchers are generally a wide band, which starts just under the bust and ends right below the belly button. They can either have a hook closure or be a single piece. This girdle is especially helpful to create that desired hourglass shape. It will help flatten out the abdomen, as well. The waist cincher works well with form-fitting dresses, pencil skirts, and form-fitting blouses. Wide width belts can be used as waist cinchers in addition to, or in place of, the regular foundation you would wear. A fantastic thing about the wide width belt is that it draws attention to the waist, so your cinched-in waist becomes the focal point of the outfit.

One piece slip suit – This piece is basically a camisole and high waist short combined, and it gives the ultimate support. I call these ones "the big guns." Bring this girdle out when you wear your most form fitting dresses. It minimizes the bust, flattens out the tummy, slims down the hips, and smoothes out the appearance of cellulite. Another advantage is that since it is a one piece suit there are no panty lines. None! You can't see where it starts or where it ends. It does an excellent job of flattening out and smoothing down, but if you want to get that extra "oomph" you can add a waist cincher on top to bring the waist in a little more. The slip suit & cincher combo is not for the faint at heart (or those with weak lungs!) Bring out this combo when you need to really perfect your body shape.

Corselet – Corselets combine both the high waist panty girdle and the bra, all in one. They generally have a stomach panel to flatten the stomach and offer bust support in the bra portion of the garment.

Body slips – Body slips can create excellent curves. Be cautious when selecting a Body slip as your foundation, though, because if you have ample hips and thighs they can slide up as you walk, making for an uncomfortable situation. Body slips are best worn by the apple and the upside–down triangle shapes.

Corsets - *A* great corset can dramatically define the waist and give the torso the look of utter perfection. However, corsets with plastic boning are more for recreation than for practical usage. Hips and Curves, an online plus-size lingerie one-stop shop, actually offers corsets with steel boning. Steel boning is the best option if you want a functional corset. Corsets with the steel boning can be a little pricey, but they will keep their shape and will last for years and years.

When buying your shapewear, you'll need to consider several things. Think about your body type, your problem areas, and the needs of your wardrobe. It is optimal that women have different pieces for their different needs. Your foundation arsenal should consist of one special occasion and one basic everyday foundation piece at a minimum. Add different specialty foundations to your collection over time to ensure that you will be able to handle any wardrobe challenge.

Brassieres, a.k.a. the bra

I rarely see a woman without a bra on, but I do want to talk about bras as it relates to wearing the proper size, knowing when to replace them, and knowing what kind to buy that will compliment your "girls" and keep them high and proud.

First off, *go in for a bra fitting from your local lingerie store.* They are both painless and free! Bra fittings should be done once every six months to account for any weight gain or weight loss. There are many women walking around with the wrong bra on. You have probably seen the "muffin breast" phenomenon, which is created by a too-small cup size. And contrary to popular male belief, spilling over is not very sexy, nor is your bust becoming lost in a cup size too big, either. Fittings take about 5 minutes and once you have on the right size bra, you will feel so much better, look great, and be much more comfortable.

Every girl should have a 5-way strapless convertible bra. This bra can literally work with every type of neckline imaginable—from asymmetrical, to strapless, halter, and crisscross. Some of these bras even have clear straps that connect the bra in the back in case you have a top with a low back. Often I hear women with large breasts skip the strapless bra, citing that it won't hold their breasts up. The invention of clear straps helps bustier woman go strapless. The Jill Scott Butterfly Bra from Ashley Stewart not only helps the bustier woman wear strapless garments, but the sides of the bra come up so far that it gets all the underarm side fat. This is one of those small victories that can make any woman's day.

A minimizing bra can be a good thing. This particular bra can help reduce the excessively busty look of a woman with ample breasts. Now you might be asking, why would I want to make them look smaller? A minimizer is great for those times that you need to be modest, like church, work, places with children, etc. Think about the girl with the super curvy derriere that goes to her place of worship with a super tight skirt on. There are just some places where modesty counts. In critical situations, this can add that extra touch of class to your reputation as a lady.

A good bra can give any girl an extra boost of confidence. With your boobies perky and in the right place, your back posture improves. So wear your breasts, big or small, the right way with pride. The fit of your bra can be the major difference in whether you look frumpy or fabulous, so it is well worth the extra effort to make sure they're supported correctly.

Tips for wearing foundation garments, girdle, and bras

Above anything, before you get suited up, use the ladies' room. There is nothing worse than getting everything on and having to take everything off to use the restroom. Some foundations do come with "pee holes," but do yourself a favor and just take off the entire thing if you've gotta go. Trust me, you'll be glad you did.

Assess the shaping requirements of the outfit you are wearing and choose your foundation garment accordingly. Are you wearing strapless? Is your dress form fitting? Is the material thin? What little bulges do you need to smooth out for this particular outfit? These are all questions that you need to ask yourself when deciding what foundation to wear with your ensemble. Once you have answered these questions, pick the shapewear in your arsenal that works best.

Foundation garments, girdles and bras do not last forever. I used to work in a certain plus-size store in college and we used to do bra fittings for the customers. You would not believe the state of women's bras. You name it; I have seen it, from hanging on by a thread to a missing or broken underwire. Your bust—large or small—will never look its best under such shabby conditions. Foundation garments and the like need to be replaced every 6 to 12 months, depending on how much wash-and-wear they get. To extend their life, *don't* toss them in the dryer with everything else. After a time, this will effectively bake the spandex, and they'll lose their stretchy shaping power.

When buying a girdle, try on your size first, then go down a size...only if necessary. Women automatically default to buying the girdle that is too small, because they think it will make them look slimmer. Buying a girdle that is undersized can actually cause the girdle to roll down, resulting in the bubble-thigh look, or even worse, cause the greatest pain you have ever felt in your life. You also would not want to buy a girdle that is too large, as it won't fulfill its maximum shaping potential. Go for the foundation garment that is your size first, if you feel it isn't providing the support you need, then go down a size or two until you sense that the foundation is accomplishing its purpose. Spanx, the Cacique sections of Lane Bryant and Hips and Curves online have a plus-size lingerie department that can satisfy all your foundation and lingerie needs. I am very excited about *any* place that I can get a good quality bra, a firm girdle, and even some sexy lingerie. In your trips to places like these, remember these tricks of the trade to ensure you are armed and ready for war. The *fashion* war, that is.

Chapter 4

Shopaholics Anonymous

Curvy ladies, you know from experience that our options are limited when we go out to clothing stores. I don't want to hear any complaining about it. Although the fashionable options are limited, they are still dramatically better than they used to be. I read blog after blog complaining about the lack of this, and the lack of that. There are not that many plus-size clothing lines and designers out there. So when you find one that you like, by all means, support them! Here are a few tips that should have your closet the envy of your friends and keep the plus-size shopping blues away!

Quality over Quantity – It is far better to have a closet with just few pieces that are well made with quality fabric because they will last you for years. Low quality clothes will cost you more money in the long run, because eventually they will be rendered unwearable, either through wear, shrinkage, or malfunction. Buying a quality garment, provided that you care for it properly, can last 5 years or more. I have several quality pieces that have had a special place in my wardrobe for close to a decade. Consider these particular pieces your long-term fashion investments.

When going shopping, don't expect to find an entire fabulous wardrobe in one trip. Try to keep your mind from getting caught up in the idea that you need to buy an outfit or even a single piece every time you go out. Don't set yourself up for disappointment.

If you find something that looks amazing on you, buy it! Do not leave it in the store for some other woman to claim, because you know once you leave, it'll be gone forever. And then you have to think about that dress that you should have bought and didn't for all of perpetuity.

Keep a dress in reserve. Last-minute shopping is a personal pet peeve of mine. As a curvy girl stylist, I have had client after client call me on Wednesday and tell me they need a dress for an event on Saturday. Even as a stylist it is very difficult to come up with the perfect dress virtually overnight. Now, imagine the average woman trying to accomplish this. Rushed or hasty decisions generally leave you with an outfit that you only feel lukewarm about, and doesn't make you look your radiant best. So save yourself the heartache and always be on the hunt for your reserve dress—the dress you have on hand in case your best shopping efforts before a special occasion prove to be fruitless.

Create your wardrobe around your best feature. Everyone has that feature that they love about themselves. It could be your sexy shoulders, your long neck, your beautiful legs, or your enviable bust. Once you figure out what your best feature is, dress and accessorize to accentuate it.

Look for heavy fabrics – Heavy fabrics are more forgiving to the figure than thin ones. They can conceal imperfections much better than thin, flimsy fabrics, particularly for tailored pieces. Distinguishing heavy fabrics is as easy as holding your clothes up to a light and determining the relative amount of transparency.

Incorporate structured pieces in your wardrobe – Not everything has to be made of stretch jersey knit. I know jersey knit is comfortable, but clothes that are structured and tailored to fit look more sophisticated and convey a bit more panache. Don't give in to the fact that the vast majority of plus-size clothes are made of jersey knit—you can shop your way around it!

Natural fabrics look best – Cotton, wool, and silk are examples of fabrics to look for when you're shopping. They will last longer, keep their shape, and stay looking their best when washed or dry cleaned.

Look at the garment size and fit, not the size tag – Okay, say it with me: "Screw what size the tag says!" At over 250 pounds I have clothes in my closet from a straight size large and up. Assess the garment's width and style. Remember that even though something may not fit the way the designer intended, this doesn't mean it can't work for you in a different way. If the piece fits and looks great on you then go for it. And on the flip side, don't buy a piece just because you like the way it looks on the rack and it has your size tag in it. You ladies all know that the "correct number" is not a fit guarantee.

Be creative - Assess the different pieces in your shopping trip that you like best. Can they be altered to work for you? For our curvy girls with some sewing skills, ask yourself is this might even be a do-it-yourself project. This can be done especially when shopping in the "skinny girl" section. You can take those dresses and turn them into tops with just a quick, simple hem.

Don't invest too much in trendy pieces - Trendy clothes come and go from season to season. Remember those Timberland Manolo boots? Would you even be caught dead in them now? It's probably safe to say no. Spend wisely on trend-driven pieces because in a season or two they will fall into the "absolutely do not wear ever again" section of your closet. Do have fun with select, affordable trendy pieces, combining them with your quality wardrobe basics.

Pick and choose your trends to work with your figure– Go ahead and try on the trends that you like in the dressing room. See if they work for you, and do not let how they look on others play into the decision of whether you should purchase the item in question. This year I bought harem pants with full knowledge that they were not made for my body type. Now they are collecting dust in my closet, because it would cost me more to ship them back.

Online Shopping

The great, glorious world-wide-web is the single place where you can find the widest range of plus-size clothing. Even department stores like Neiman Marcus and Nordstrom have a much better selection online than they do in their stores. Don't be afraid of online shopping. If you know your measurements, you can compare them to the size charts provided on the websites and you should be able to decipher what size to purchase. No one likes to return by mail, and returning items abroad can be an utter nightmare, so just be a little careful. You might want to test out online plus clothing companies by first purchasing a sale item, so you can check out the quality of the clothing.

Another great way of finding clothes from online stores and boutiques is to read clothing reviews. As a blogger, I often find myself looking for reviews on different retailers to find out both general opinions and opinions on specific items. Retailer websites themselves often offer customer reviews of items which can offer further insight to help you make your decision.

Online shopping also opens up international avenues to obtain styles and pieces that are not offered in your immediate area. By using a simple size conversion chart, you can easily figure out what size you wear in clothes from the UK, Europe, or wherever. A simple Google search can also help you convert US dollars to Pounds, Euros, or any other currency.

European/UK/USA Size Conversion Chart

UK	14	16	18	20	22	24	26	28	30	32
EURO	42	44	46	48	50	52	54	56	58	60
USA	10	12	14	16	18	20	22	24	26	28

Now that you've accumulated some online shopping wisdom, let me share with you some of my favorite online shops. Here's a list of the places I shop online and why I like them.

Asos – With a new roster of extended sizes for the curvy girl, they have a lot of nice garments, but their trench coats really stand out. Their trenches are simple and chic, with just a touch of special detailing to make the other girls envious. (They're UK-based, too.)

Shop: *asos.com*

Dorothy Perkins – I shop Dorothy Perkins for those trendy pieces that I want to incorporate in my wardrobe for a relatively low cost. Dorothy Perkins is a store based in the United Kingdom, but it does ship to the United States. Their sizes go up to a UK size 22 (the equivalent of US size 18).

Shop: *dorothyperkins.com*

eShakti – This company has also been around for a while, but they have definitely kicked up their design aesthetic over the past year. This retailer has garments that range from ethnic glam to sassy chic. One of the best things about this retailer is that you get a high quality garment for a great price.

Shop: *eshakti.com*

Etsy – This website is a great portal to find some remarkable independent designers. Etsy shopping can ensure that you achieve a style all your own by finding pieces that can be considered one of a kind in your home area. Although most of designers with shops on Etsy only go up to a size 14, a lot of them do offer custom sizing. You may have to pay extra for the fabric, but it will be well worth it in the end.

If you find an independent designer you love that offers to custom-create a garment based on your measurements, seize the opportunity! When taking advantage of custom sizing, remember to mention to the designer any extremes in your measurements, like long arms, a wide hip span, short torso, big knees and so on. Talk to the designer about your body type—this will help you end up with the fit that you want.

Shop: *etsy.com*

Evans – This is another UK-based retailer. The thing I like about Evans is that they have worked with singers like Chaka Khan and Beth Ditto on creating their own clothing lines.

Shop: *evans.co.uk*

Igigi – This website is my go-to place for chic work wear. A couple of my very favorite skirts have come from Igigi. This label helps you have a polished look every time you head into the office.

Shop: *igigi.com*

Jibri – I particularly adore this designer because she incorporates unique, classic feminine silhouettes with a high-end design aesthetic. She uses quality materials and all of the garments I own from her exhibit great work(wo)manship. What's better? She offers custom pieces. (No trips to the alterations shop!) Jibri offers plus-size designs in sizes 14 – 24.

See it: *jibrionline.com*
Shop: *etsy.com/shop/jibrionline*

La'Dan's Closet – Fashionable as they are warm, Ladan's Closet's stylish outerwear is perfect for the cold winter months. Ladan's Closet provides the go-to winter coat essentials.

Shop: *la-danscloset.com*

Monif C – This designer has been around for some time now, gracing BET's Rip the Runway for several years. She is famous for her convertible dresses, but is now becoming even more famous (and I might add adored) for providing fashionable bathing suits for the curvy girl. These swimsuits are hot too, definitely not the grandma suits that we are all used to seeing in plus-size departments.

Shop: *monifc.com*

Nordstrom – Lets face it, the in-store options usually aren't so hot. However, the selection of pieces and designers are significantly better online.

Shop: *nordstrom.com*

Ralph Lauren – Great for basics, Ralph Lauren has always been one my favorites for his distinctly American aesthetic. His plus-size collection always harbors great staples for any curvy girl's closet.

Shop: *ralphlauren.com*

Boutique Shopping

Plus-size boutiques seem to be popping up everywhere. I love the boutique shopping experience in general, but love it more when I can find a store that caters to plus-size exclusively. They are still few and far between, but when I am visiting a new city, a simple internet search will let me know if there is a boutique in my area. If you plan to visit one, always call in advance to verify they are still open. Boutique shopping is always a little more expensive than typical shopping, so be prepared. The service that you get at such places is well worth it. Boutiques are a great place to check out those pieces that you have only seen online. These boutiques often pick up independent designers and labels like Igigi, Monif C, and Jibri. Even if you don't find anything to take home with you, you can still examine the style, quality, and fabrics from various designers and determine if you would like to purchase pieces from them in the future.

Thrift store, Consignment, and Vintage Shopping

One-of-a-kind pieces can definitely be treasure-hunted for at thrift stores. The good thing about thrift shopping is that you can be almost certain that know one will have what you'll be wearing at your next soiree. Don't be shy or embarrassed about setting foot in a thrift store—you have *this* stylist's *full* approval to do so. And when you're hunting for that fabulous thrift item, keep these things in mind.

Be creative with thrift store merchandise. Since you pay minimally for the item purchased—sometimes only 1 or 2 dollars—you can cut, hem, slice, and dice your new purchase without worrying about wasting your money. So what if you accidentally ruined it in your creative attempt? It was literally just two bucks. Hooray for that!

Don't be confined to plus-size thrift stores. Think back about 15 years. Plus-size clothes were made almost strictly for older people. The plus-size industry has made monumental strides in the last 5 years. So vintage plus-size thrift stores may be low on the stylish pieces, because plus size just got some fashionable pieces in the last 5 to 10 years. Venture to some regular thrift stores.

Dry clean or wash all of your items from the thrift store before wearing. You have no idea where these clothes were before you got them, and they'll probably have that distinctive, but mysterious thrift store smell.

Check to make sure the fabric isn't ruined with water-log or dry-rot. This can easily be checked with a simple sniff test and a keen eye. I think everyone knows what water-log or mildew smells like.

High-end consignment shops are a wonderful place to find spendy-looking fashion accessories. The advantage to shopping high end consignment is that the owners of these boutiques generally approve all the pieces placed in the store. These boutiques consist of new, nearly new, or gently used clothing, shoes, and accessories.

Vintage shopping is not as hard as it looks. Now before you start casually tossing around the word vintage, know that vintage clothes are considered to be clothes that are at least between 20 to 30 years old. This means at a minimum the clothes have to have come from 1990 or before. So just because you bought something from a thrift store does not mean it's vintage. Most places that carry vintage clothes are clearly defined as vintage and it is very obvious from the clothing that they have: jumpsuits from the '70s, Members Only jackets from the '80s, and all the poly-blend grooviness you can stand.

Vintage shopping is not always equivalent to cheap shopping. I have happened across Oscar de la Renta shades that retail for $100 in a vintage shop and a Halston dress for $88. Vintage clothing can sell for thousands of dollars.

When shopping thrift, consignment, and vintage I am generally on the hunt for sweater dresses, shirt dresses, dresses with a flared skirt, embellished cardigans, and funky blazers. These pieces, whether in regular sizes or plus sizes, are the easiest to fit the curvy girl. You don't have to stick strictly to looking for these pieces, but this is a great way to start off your hunt and increase the probability of finding a garment to add to your closet.

"Skinny Girl Shopping"

Don't restrict yourself exclusively to plus-size shopping. With the trends of clothing being oversized, it can be very easy for a curvy girl to shimmy into that top or dress from the straight-size department. The designer may have intended an article of clothing to be worn one way, but this does not mean you can't wear it another way. In the dressing room, give yourself an honest assessment on how the garment fits and if it complements your body. Search for items that have stretch, have a full skirt, and oversized pieces. Wear your girdle when you're "skinny girl shopping," because there is a good chance that the stretchy items are going to be the pieces that will work. Wearing a girdle will allow you to see in the store whether the item is going to flatter or if it will not work. Here are some tips:

Buy two and take it to a seamstress. If you just can't live your life without that fabulous dress you just spotted in the window of one of the hottest boutiques, buy two, take them to your local tailor and see if she can make a chic little frock that will work for you. Be prepared not to get the exact replication of the dress, but with the assistance of a skillful seamstress, you will come close.

If it doesn't work, it just doesn't work. Don't get frustrated, just move on to the next store. Remember these clothes aren't meant to fit you, so if you find a piece that does, just consider it an added bonus to life.

Don't be intimidated. Some women won't even walk into a store that isn't plus-sized because they are afraid of what the sales girl is thinking. Well who gives a whit? It's just like strolling into Versace even though you may only have $100 in your bank account. So what! You are limiting your options if you only shop in one particular type of store.

Department Stores & Plus-Size Retailer Shopping

Department stores and plus-size retailers offer a one stop shop for finding apparel that fit plus-sizes. Although they may lack in exceptional or unique styles, they are still great places to buy staples like jeans and blazers. But beware of shopping too much at one particular retailer; it can make you look like their spokesperson (which isn't good, if you're not getting paid for the gig). Diversify your wardrobe. Pick pieces from here and there.

An advantage to department store shopping is that they have many high-end plus designers as well as designers who have extended their lines to include plus-size, like Calvin Klein, Michael Kors, and Ralph Lauren. Here you can potentially find nice structured and tailored pieces, which give off a polished look.

Bridal/Bridesmaid Shops

This is probably the best kept secret to finding a gorgeous dress on short notice. Bridal shops, such as David's Bridal, is stocked full of dresses that go up as high as a size 26. The key to shopping at a bridal store is sticking to your innate taste. No one wants to paint the town red in what appears to be a bridesmaid dress. Instead, look at the dresses and ask yourself, does this scream bridesmaid? If you're still not sure, these tips should help you avoid the bridal party look:

Steer clear of overly large bows.
Replace that waist sash with a belt.
Don't choose a full length dress, unless you are attending a black tie event.
Avoid pastel colors for your dress.
Pass up on the piece with the floral attachments.

Low-End Shopping

The best thing about shopping in places like Target and Wal-Mart are that they are often picking up mainstream designers, who design a more affordable clothing line specifically for these stores. Designers, like Jean Paul Gaultier, Norma Kamali, and Isaac Mizrahi have graced the women's departments of America's favorite mega stores. These designers generally only have sizes that go up to a size 14 or 16, but depending on the make and material of their clothing, a curvy girl can incorporate them into her wardrobe. Norma Kamali at Wal-mart goes up to an XXL and the pieces are so similar to her high-end line it's scary. Just be on the lookout for clothes that didn't translate well from high end to low end. In those circumstances they can look terribly cheap and unflattering. Don't get caught up in the excitement of being able to buy a certain designer if the clothes are hideous, because then you will end up with a collection of rubbish you won't wear.

If you take nothing else from this chapter keep the following points in mind. Do not limit yourself to one particular place to shop. Different types of shops can serve as inspiration for new outfit ideas. Try thrift stores, online shopping, department stores, independent boutiques, etc. This will allow you to create your own looks and not appear like you buy all of your clothes from one place. Plus-size shopping is about being inventive and spending some time pulling together a fabulous look from virtually nothing.

Chapter 5

Accessories and the City

Accessories are a powerful component to any girl's outfit. And accessories, for the most part, do not discriminate based on size. It is one of the few areas in fashion where the playing field is even. Using accessories properly can take you from day wear to evening wear with something as simple as the change of a bag. The right accessories can even launch your winter wardrobe straight into spring without a second thought. As a curvy girl, accessories are a great way to enjoy fashion's variety and abundance.

Sunglasses

Take your look up a few notches with glammed out shades. The big, Jackie O style sunglasses are a staple when you're going for style and sophistication; simply no other option will do.

To look your best in your shades, buy the sunglasses that best complement your face shape. Round and oval faces should lean towards a frame with rectangle or square shapes. This will bring out the angles in your face. Square faces will benefit from a rounder frame to bring out the curves and contours. Heart shaped faces tend to have a larger forehead so they should select a rectangular or octagonal casing.

Shoes

Manolos just may not be for the big girl. While in the department store I was trying to pick up a pair of Manolos. This was my first time trying these shoes on. What I found out that day was one important thing, all sizes aren't created equal even if different shoes have the same numerical size.

A lot of curvy girls can only wear a large sized or a wide width shoe, which can make their stylish shoe options severely limited. Forcing your foot into a shoe that just doesn't work isn't the answer, either. Foot roll-over and spillage looks hideous, no matter how cute the shoe. Different style shoes are made different ways, and so some are cut a bit wider than others. Find a shoe designer or retailer that works well for you. I am personally a Nine West fan, because the shoes have a decent width and they have size 11 and 12. Some plus-size retailers are also starting to carry shoes, like Torrid. Torrid's shoes are actually made to accommodate a slightly wider foot. Some higher-end designers carry a wider shoe and some don't, you just have to find the right designers for your feet.

Shoes can be the magic spark of any outfit. They can take a plain black dress and make it exciting. Essential colors that every woman should have in her wardrobe are black, gold, and nude. The essential styles that you should have include:

Ballet flats – This shoe allows you to be comfortable and cute at the same time. Great for the office or a casual Saturday date.

Peep-toe pumps – Covered up enough for the office, but that tiny peep gives everyone the lovely view of your nicely manicured feet. The peep-toe, depending on your outfit, can go to the office or out dancing.

Flat dressy sandals – This shoe is an alternative to the flat for the summer.

Mid-level pumps - This is the shoe that you actually walk in all day and is great for places where you are going to be standing and mingling, or places where you will be doing some extensive walking. This shoe offers comfort paired with the sexiness of a heel.

Booties – Fun for the winter, but with a peep toe they can be transferred to be able to be worn in all seasons. Reserve your suede booties for the winter, and let your leather or patent leather ones be free game all year.

Knee high boots – This is one of the biggest shoe difficulties for the curvy girl— particularly finding a boot wide enough to fit her calf. To get around this problem, check out retailers who sell plus-size boots like Lane Bryant, Torrid, and Evans. Also, *6pm.com* and *zappos.com* even allow you to do a search of plus-size boots on their website. An alternative to the all-leather boot is a boot that has knit sweater material on the upper shaft, which can be very stylish and you won't have to buy in plus-size.

Casual Sneakers – Besides your gym sneakers, you need a sneaker that you can actually use for a picnic in the park. I love Converse for this reason. They even come in pink! You can wear your Converse, leggings, and a nice open cardigan with a tank and still look cute.

The show-stopper shoe – This is my favorite shoe of all. This is the shoe that may be the trendiest shoe of the year. A shoe that is so seductively high that you have to wear it in extreme moderation. This shoe gets you all the compliments. People will be dying to know where you got it. This shoe takes your outfit up to rock star level. Bring out this shoe when you really want to pull out all the stops.

Belts

Belts go in and out of style all the time, but regardless of the trends, a belt is a crucial part of any girl's wardrobe. They add shape and create curve. Belts can act like a corset or a cincher in the waist department, forming a clearly defined waistline. The key to wearing a belt is wearing it so that it flatters your particular body type. Some body types have it easier than others when it comes to adding this accessory, but everyone can wear it one way or another.

Let's talk about the "don'ts" of wearing a belt first. One of the mistakes I see time and time again among plus-size women is wearing a flimsy belt if your stomach is where you carry most of your weight. This pertains to my apple shapes, mostly. A thin, flimsy belt will get lost in the folds in your body. Choose a structured belt made of leather, faux leather or any other type of material that won't lose its shape.

Belts are easiest to wear for women who are pear-shaped or hourglass-shaped, but this does not mean if you don't have this body type that you cannot accomplish this flattering look. You should wear the belt slightly beneath the bust line or at the natural waistline. This draws attention to the natural curvy figure that you have.

If you lack definition in your midsection add the belt on top of a flared skirt or dress. If your natural waistline just won't accommodate a belt, try wearing it just underneath your bust at the location of an empire waist seam. This will give the illusion of curvature. When wearing the belt at the empire position, be aware that belts should not make you look pregnant! Body types with some extra stomach may have issues with this. If so, try wearing a belt on different parts of your waist. You can try wearing it above, right on, or just below your natural waistline. If that doesn't work, opt for a different kind of dress or skirt. Try an A-line dress or a flared skirt.

The box & the upside down triangle-shaped ladies tend to have difficulty making a belt look good on their figures. These ladies should look for a belt around 3 to 4 inches in width and pull tight. (You should still be able to breathe, though!) The belt will act as a bit of a corset, pulling in the waist. On straight silhouettes, choose flared skirts to pair with a belt, too. For the boyish-shaped lady....this means ladies with more of a straight silhouette (or a smaller than average waist to hip ratio) wear a belt on your hips. It is more of a bohemian look, but it will actually look very chic when worn the right way.

If you are petite, choose a smaller, skinnier belt. In essence, your torso is so short a belt that is four inches wide can literally cover your entire stomach, cutting you in half and making you look shorter. Pick belts that agree more with your size. A medium to skinny belt will do.

Above all, have fun with your belts! They are a great way to break up monotony of an outfit and have a polished look. I have people ask me all the time where I get my belts from. Honestly, most of my belts come from Target. They go up to a XXL and can accommodate even a large waist. If you don't believe me just go out and try. Try adding a colorful or patterned belt that is unexpected. The color of your belt doesn't necessarily have to match your outfit— the colors just need to complement each other.

Purses & Bags

I have always thought that the purses that women carry are a window into their soul, or at least their personalities. A bag can tell you so much about a woman, how girly they are, their taste, if they are eclectic, and so on. So picking the right bags to represent you is very important. While the styles of bags we carry may be different, there are two structures of bags that are necessary for every stylish girl.

The hobo/satchel is a bag that you can literally carry your life in. This bag also has the potential to make you look slimmer. I say the bigger the better when carrying this sort of purse. Your body will look small next to this extra large purse. And just as a rule of thumb, avoid those extra small purses. When over your shoulder, they can make your arms (and you, for that matter,) look enormous. I never carry a bag smaller than my thigh to ensure that I have the size that will compliment me best.

A beautiful clutch is an elegant transformation, swiftly taking your look from day to night. Clutches are appropriate for going out at night, weddings, and black tie events. Play up your outfit with clutches that feature luxurious embellishments, ruffles, and beading. Wonderful places to find these sassy little treasures are vintage shops. You can find clutches made of metal, wood, or other non-traditional materials.

Jewelry

You can look like a fashionista who really *knows* by knowing *what* to add and *how much* to wear. Moderation in any situation is always a smart way to approach accessorizing with jewelry. The "Christmas tree approach" to adorning yourself will have people confused when they look at you. They won't know where to look! They will be bouncing back and forth between your bracelet, ring, necklace, earrings, watch, anklet, and toe ring. Just thinking about it can make a girl tired!

A good way to approach your jewelry accessorizing is to choose a statement piece of jewelry to center your look around. It can be any piece of jewelry, a huge cuff, sparkling chandelier earrings, a bibbed necklace, and so on. After you have decided on what conversation piece, look at the region of the body it's on. If it is on the shoulders or above, then think about adding something below the shoulders, like a ring or bracelet. If it is on the arms or wrists, add something to the neck or ears. No one woman needs a huge bibbed necklace on and a pair of huge chandelier earrings—opt for the studs instead. It's been said a million times, but Coco Chanel hit the nail on the head when she said, "when accessorizing, always take off the last thing you put on." It definitely keeps you from going overboard.

Maintaining a bountiful stash of accessories is the way I live my life, but at the very least a girl should have these pieces in her jewelry box:

Diamond earring studs – Whether synthetic stones or the real deal, a pair of diamond earrings is the quintessential way to show simple, quiet elegance. This earring, although generally small, can always give that dazzle.

Pearls – A pearl necklace and earring set gives that look of class and sophistication. I'm a southern girl at heart, so I literally have about eight different versions of pearls. Every woman that I see in a pearl necklace reminds me of the poise and class of Charlotte from *Sex and the City*.

A ring with a large colored center – It can add a splash of color to even the grayest monotone of outfits.

Chandelier earrings – These earrings are super glamorous, and with the right pair, old Hollywood can be brought into your look.

A *bangle* – This is not referring to those multitudes of bangles that make all that clickety clack noise as you move your arms. A classic bangle, whether costume, platinum, or silver, can easily transition from the grocery store to a night on the town.

A watch – A nice grown-up looking watch can add an extra touch of professionalism to your look. My preference is a watch made of stainless steel, but a gold or leather-banded watch will do nicely also.

Scarves

Scarves are a simple solution for adding color and drama to a look. With a multitude of ways to tie and wear a scarf, you can use it to convey the mood you are in. These five ways to wear a scarf will have you bringing the excitement wherever you go.

Want a look that is *tres, tres chic*? Wrap your scarf around your head and then fling it over the shoulders and pair it with your darkest sunglasses.

Feeling like a Parisian, start off with your scarf draped over your shoulders and then throw one of the ends over your shoulder for a look that is magnifique!

For that London bloke look, tie your scarf in a slip knot. Fold the scarf in half, then hang the halved scarf over your shoulder. Next, proceed to slip the scarf through the loop. Add your London Fog coat and you are ready to roam the streets in London, or anywhere else for that matter, in style.

Looking for a more traditional look? Wrap the scarf around the neck once and let the loose ends rest in the front.

Want to impress your associates with a sign of true old-school sophistication? Wear the scarf in the ascot style. Wrap the scarf around the neck, same way as mentioned above, with the loose ends hanging in the front. After that, proceed to the tie the loose ends. Feeling posh yet?

Hosiery

Almost considered the lifeline for my entire fall/winter wardrobe, colored tights (and even plain old black tights) not only look amazing, but they can easily take your dresses and skirts from spring to fall and winter with ease. Please don't add tights to your sundresses, though. However, adding tights to a black shirt dress or a floral skirt, for example, can winterize many of your spring pieces. My favorite place for color hosiery is none other than We Love Colors (www.welovecolors.com).They offer plus-size tights and leggings in every color imaginable. They even have some great print tights and fishnets.

Less is more when adorning yourself with accessories. One step too far and you can look like a gypsy. Use these simple rules and tips to create the perfect accessorized look. And remember, a girl can never *own* too many accessories, only wear too many at once!

Chapter 6

Tips for the Curvy Girl

In this chapter I want to help the average curvy girl with some tricks that I have learned along the way. This includes such fashion tips as how to keep dry under your girdle to the best way to get over the tired face blues and so on. This chapter is centered on everyday situations that I have encountered as a fashionable plus-size woman.

Personal Maintenance

Do not, and I repeat, do not relinquish looking your best because you are in a weight loss transition. Personally, I have been losing weight since I have been 12 years old. The point of me saying this is that so many times I know women who will not buy clothes to fit their "right now" body because they are waiting for their weight loss train to come in. This is not to say that I am advocating against taking care of your body, but I am advocating against looking like a hot mess while you are in your transition. Buying an entire new wardrobe isn't necessary every time you lose 20 pounds either. Your tailor can help you alter your clothes, so they fit you while you are losing weight.

Monistat Chafing Powder Gel is your BFF. – Wearing foundation garments, especially in the summertime, can cause chafing and heat rashes, especially in the unmentionable areas. Unfortunately, it's just part of being a curvy girl. To help keep dry try Monistat Powder Gel. This product goes on like a gel but dries silky smooth. It helps to prevent, sooth, and heal heat rashes. A couple weeks of using this product and I have gotten rid of my summertime rashes completely.

Employ your deodorant to keep dry in more places than just under your arms. Deodorant keeps you nice and dry. If your thighs are rubbing together and a bit sweaty, you can rub deodorant between them. This goes too for ladies with large breasts or any "creases" that can sweat during the warmer months. A quick swipe underneath the bust or between the legs can have you sitting a lot more comfortably when it is blazing outside. Also, you can apply deodorant to the bottom of your feet to keep them from sweating if that's a particular problem.

Carry an extra pair of panties in your purse. We are all adults here and let's admit that accidents happen. An extra pair of panties will give you a sense of security and a backup, so that when something does happen you are prepared.

A small bottle of cuticle oil can give your feet an emergency makeover. It will revive your hands and feet, get rid of any visible dryness, and give you the look of a fresh manicure/pedicure.

A good friend told me once that you should never look like yesterday's trash. Say you had a long night of partying and you wake up, see that your reflection scares you, but you need to look presentable in a hurry. If your hair is full of gunk from last night's hairstyle use a hair freshener. I use Bumble and Bumble's Prep. It doubles as a prep before you fix your hair, but also as a freshener to help release smells that your hair maybe holding and to loosen up any holding products.

The whiter your eyes are, the less tired you look. Visine Clear Eyes is great for revitalizing tired eyes. I know I sound like the commercial, but it works.

Be a lady. One of the biggest components of style is behavior. Namely, acting like a lady. Have manners and show class, no matter how much money is in your bank account. If this is something you have never been taught or need some brushing up on, pick up a book from your local library. I keep a book by on my nightstand called *Better than Beauty* by Helen Valentine & Alice Thompson. It was originally published in 1938 and even though it is quite dated, much of the advice is still very relevant. Charm is something that never goes out of style.

Clothing Care

You have invested in your clothing, so now you'll want to take care of your pieces and make sure the money that you have invested doesn't go to waste. Tips in this section will help you keep your clothes looking like new, while keeping their shape.

Read the clothing care labels. The best way to find out how to care for your clothes is to read the label on the clothing and follow the instructions. If you do not follow the instructions, be prepared for the consequences.

Find a separate place for the clothing that can't be washed. I've actually ruined quite a few expensive pieces by accidentally washing them when they're mixed in with the rest of my laundry. For some reason I have an issue with wool. I have washed, dried, and shrank so many wool garments, not because I didn't follow instructions, but because these pieces got tossed in with my regular laundry. You will save yourself a lot of heartache if you just set aside a place for your dry cleaning and special instruction garments.

Dry cleaning is the way to go. Dry cleaning is my favorite way to clean my wardrobe essentials. It keeps your clothes looking newer for much longer, but beware of a few things first. If you have an item in which you suspect the color might bleed, have the dry cleaner test the fabric first. Most dry cleaners have a rule that if your clothes bleed it is not their fault and you will not be reimbursed for your garment. Most dry cleaners will sew on missing buttons for free, so take advantage of that, since you are already paying for the service.

Dry clean the cheap clothes too. Synthetic materials, like rayon, can go to the cleaner's, too. Some feel that if your clothes were cheap then you shouldn't take them to the cleaner, but I say no to that. If you like the garment, cheap or not, try to take care of it so it will last.

A seamstress or tailor is a very necessary person to have in your life. Alterations can turn an okay looking garment into a fabulous one. Fit is everything. When you find an excellent tailor or seamstress, stick with them. They will know your body type and your measurements and can alter your clothing accordingly. The best relationship you can make for your fashion future is with your tailor.

Woolite is the bomb! For dark clothes that are washable, you definitely don't want them to fade or lose their shape. So put Woolite in your machine instead of the usual detergent. I have tried all the specialty detergents and Woolite has always kept my clothes looking newer longer.

Skip the fabric softener on your darks. It will cause your clothes to fade faster.

Do not dry your shapewear or bras. Drying your shapewear and bras will shorten the life of your foundations. The dryer will heat up and eventually weaken the elastic over time.

Wash your jeans inside out, tie the legs together, and air dry them to keep them from fading. If you are worried about water-log, put them on the air fluff cycle of your dryer or give them an extra spin in the spin cycle to dispense of excess water.

Be prepared with baby wipes. To keep makeup from staining your clothes or from just plain out embarrassing you, use baby wipes stashed in your purse to remove or at least reduce the visibility of the stain. Baby wipes can also assist with shoe stains.

Keep a sewing kit in your purse. A sewing kit can save you in a time of crisis, such as a ripped seam, a button that just fell off, and anything else that can a happen to your clothing. You do not have to be an expert to sew a button or mend a seam. Yes, you may want to get the problem fixed professionally eventually, but for that accident at the coffee shop, it is just fine.

Put some clothes on! I continually see curvy girls that are nearly naked with their breasts out and their legs out. Stop, I say! As a general rule of thumb, when my girls and I are dressing to go out, we mentally decide what we are going to show off and what we are going to cover up. For example, if you had a short skirt on, then you would wear a more modest top, and vice versa. I had a male friend tell me that the sexiest women are the ones that leave something to the imagination, and I'm inclined to agree!

Shoes

Shoes too tight? Give them a stretch. If your shoes are too tight, take them to a shoe repair shop and have them stretched. Or, stretch them the old fashioned way by wearing a pair of damp socks with them around the house.

Re-heel, re-heel, and re-heel again. Don't give up on your favorite pair of shoes. Shoe Repair shops are in reach and can be an inexpensive way to mend any worn out soles and any heel issues. I think I have literally had my favorite pair of shoes re-heeled at least 30 times. Yes, I know that I have paid more in the shoe repair shop than I did for the shoes, but it was worth it, since I know I'll never be able to buy those shoes again.

If you're out and your heel just broke, don't fret—just grab your mini tube of Superglue. Every girl should keep a small tube of Superglue in her purse to help with life's little mishaps. Apply the super glue to the heel in question and hold it to the shoe until it dries. You should try to balance most of your weight on the ball of your foot instead of the heel, but the heel should last at least until you make it home.

Have a cocktail (or two) to help to numb the pain of your very stylish pumps. I am not much of a drinker, but when I have on those pumps that just wont give you break I have a cocktail. It will at least lengthen the time you can tolerate your shoes by one to two hours. (*Of course you want to drink responsibly*)

Carry a clutch big enough to fit a thin pair of flats if you are going for a night of dancing. I learned this from a good friend who is all of 5'2 and 110 pounds. Every woman who wears heels knows our shoes hurt like hell, they just *do* after standing long enough or dancing in them. Screaming feet can ruin any girl's time, so have a back up pair of shoes just in case your feet need a rescue.

Make-Up

Pass the Milk of Magnesium, please. Sweating on the dance floor can literally sweat your makeup right off your face. Base your face with Milk of Magnesium to prevent sweat from running in your face and ruining your makeup.

A mini makeup kit should always have a special place in your purse. Say you happen to get invited to an after-work soiree and you have your work makeup still on. You know the look, just a little blush, some mascara, and a nude lip. Pack your purse with your lengthening mascara (I swear by Maybelline Intense XXL), a small compact of blush, a shimmery eye shadow, and red lip color. Since you already have your base on, this will just glam up your look just enough for the evening, having you look ever-so-fabulous and well-prepared.

Some Parting Words

A book on all the rules and tips on style would be huge, and even then, some things would still be left out. So know that just as Rome was not built in a day, great style cannot be developed in a few hours, either. But however long it takes for you to find your balance, remember that you *can* achieve great style. It is not a secret club, in which only a select few have membership. It is open to all who have the aspiration to be "a very stylish girl." You'll also have to be ready to accept that you will *not* use being plus-size as an excuse for not having great style. Without that acceptance, our adventure here will have been in vain.

If you do choose to accept the challenge, there are many benefits. Think about how you feel when you see a person with great style. You want talk to them, dress like them, and you automatically assume they have it all figured out (and that they're fabulous!) Even if they don't have it all figured out, you have already made up your mind about the person in question. This is one of those priceless advantages of good style.

As our journey comes to an end here in this crash-course manual for curvy style, I will look forward to our paths crossing again as I continue the Curvy Girl series in the future. Since I don't like goodbyes, I'll just say, see you soon! Cheers!

Resources

Boston, Lloyd. *Before you Dress: 365 Daily Tips for Her.* New York: Atria, 2005.

The Igigi website. <www.igigi.com>.

Tim Gunn's Guide to Style. TV show. <http://www.bravotv.com/tim-gunns-guide-to style>.

Mayntz, Melissa. "Buying the Perfect Swimsuit for Plus-Size Women." Essortment.com. <http://www.essortment.com/lifestyle/bu yingbuyswims_siyd.htm>.

Fluery, Mary Clare. "Cool Shades: Picking the Right Sunglasses." Washingtonian.com. 1 July 2007. Web. 20 March 2010.

"H Shape Anatomy" Myshape.com website. <http://www.myshape.com/shop/shape-anatomy/shape-h>.

Invaluable insight and knowledge from June Ambrose and Angel Garner(MUA).

Curvy boutiques here, there, and everywhere:

Curvaceous Boutique
4049 Albert Street
Regina, Saskatchewan S4S3R6
(306) 522-8789

Curvysta Boutique
1963 Hosea L. Williams
Drive Suite R104,
Atlanta, GA 30317
(877) 533-8368

Dinjii Boutique
Woodward Square
8211 Windfern Rd.
Houston, TX 77040

Kapacity Boutique
4327 Harford Rd. 2nd Floor
Lauraville, MD 21214
(443) 271.8532

K Staton Boutique
817 West 36th Street
Baltimore, MD 21211
(410)-400-9113

Lee Lee's Valise
368 Court Street

Brooklyn, NY 11231
(718) 246-5337

Lola & Gigi
92B Carrier Drive
Toronto, ON M9W 5R1
(416) 674-1077

Nikki London
520 South 4th Street
Philadelphia, PA 19147
(215) 922-3536

Pink Ginger
610 W. Crockett St.
Seattle, WA 98119
(206) 285-2629

Plush Boutique
238 Walker St, SW, Unit 10
Atlanta, GA 30313
(404) 671-8362

The Little Black Dress
1110 Tower Grove Ave
St. Louis, MO 63110
(314) 531-9990

Viva La Femme
2048 North Damen

Chicago, Illinois 60647
(773) 772.7429

Voluptuous Vixen
538 Madison St. Suite 1A
New Orleans, LA 70116
(504) 529-3588

Vintage

Redress
109 Boerum Place
Brooklyn, NY 11201
(718) 522-7962

Additional plus-size clothing websites:

Anna Scholz
www.annascholz.com

Bloomingdale's
bloomingdales.com

Cherished Woman
cherished-woman.com

Carmakoma
www.carmakoma.com

City Chic
citychiconline.com

CJ by Cookie Johnson
www.cjbycookiejohnson.com

David Meister
www.davidmeister.com

Elena Miro
www.elanmiro.com

Forever 21
forever21.com

Lafayette 148
www.lafayette148.com

La Grande Dame
lagrandedame.com

Little Woods
littlewoods.com

Macys
macys.com

Marie Denee
mariedenee.com

Melissa Masse
shop.melissamasse.com

Michael Kors
www.michaelkors.com

My Shape
myshape.com

Neiman Marcus
neimanmarcus.com

Next
www.next.co.uk

Newport News
newportnews.com

Norma Kamali
www.normakamali.com

Plum Boutique
www.pluminstyle.com

PZI Jeans
www.pzijeans.com

Saks Fifth Avenue
saksfifthavenue.com

Spanx
www.spanx.com

Spiegel
spiegel.com

Svoboda
svobodastyle.com

Talbots
www.talbots.com

We Love Colors
welovecolors.com

Yours Clothing
yoursclothing.co.uk

Upcoming Curvy Girl Books

The Curvy Teen's Guide to Style
The Curvy Girl's Guide to Shopping Abroad
The Curvy Bride's Guide to Style
The Curvy Budgetista's Guide to Style

My Blogs & Other Writing

The Curvy Girl's Guide to Style
garnerstyle.blogspot.com

Dallas Examiner for Plus-size Fashion
www.examiner.com/x-39342-Dallas-PlusSize-Fashion-Examiner#fragment-4

Have a question?

Please post your questions on style and fashion for the curvy girl to any of the above blogs in the comments section. I am very interactive with my readers and love to answer questions or hear any feedback that you may have.

My Favorite Blogs

Big Beauty
leblogdebigbeauty.com

Fashion Bomb
fashionbombdaily.com

Fatshionable
fatshionable.com

Hungry for Fashion
gabi-hungryforfashion.blogspot.com

Musings of a Fatshionista
blog.musingsofafatshionista.com

PoshGlam
poshglam.com

Saks and the City
saksinthecity.blogspot.com

The Curvy Fashionista
thecurvyfashionista.mariedenee.com